The Poverty Divide: Understanding the Struggles and Solutions

By: Tyler

Poverty Divide: Understanding the Struggles and Solutions

Global Issues, Volume 2

Thomas Ip

Published by Thomas Ip, 2024.

POVERTY DIVIDE: UNDERSTANDING THE STRUGGLES AND SOLUTIONS

First edition. April 28, 2024.

ISBN: 979-8224356591

Written by Thomas Ip.

Table of Contents

The Many Faces of Poverty

Poverty. A single word that conjures images of desperation, hunger, and lack. But the reality of poverty is far more nuanced, its face multifaceted and ever-changing. It weaves through bustling cities and remote villages, impacting millions across continents and cultures. In this chapter, we embark on a journey to understand the many faces of poverty, its definition, and its devastating consequences.

Defining the Lines: Absolute vs. Relative Poverty

At its core, poverty refers to a lack of basic necessities – food, shelter, clothing, healthcare, and education. However, measuring poverty isn't always straightforward. The most common measure is the **absolute poverty line**, established by the World Bank. This line defines extreme poverty as living on less than $1.90 (PPP - Purchasing Power Parity) per day, a bare minimum needed to meet basic needs for survival.

While the absolute poverty line provides a global benchmark, it doesn't fully capture the complexities of poverty. Enter **relative poverty**. This concept defines poverty not by a universal standard, but in relation to the average income level within a specific country or region. For example, someone earning well below the average income in a wealthy nation like the United States might be considered relatively poor, even if their income exceeds the absolute poverty line.

A Global Snapshot: The Numbers Behind the Faces

Despite economic progress, poverty remains a persistent global challenge. According to the World Bank, over 736 million people lived on less than $1.90 a day in 2015. While this number represents a significant decline from previous decades, it highlights the immense task ahead.

Poverty isn't evenly distributed. Sub-Saharan Africa remains the region with the highest poverty rates, with almost half of its population living below the absolute poverty line. South Asia comes in second, with widespread poverty particularly concentrated in rural areas.

Beyond Numbers: The Human Cost of Poverty

Statistics paint a broad picture, but the true impact of poverty lies in its relentless grip on human lives. Imagine a young girl in a war-torn country, forced to work instead of attending school. Picture a family living in a makeshift shack, struggling to find their next meal. Envision a talented artist, their creative potential stifled by the lack of resources to pursue their dreams. These are the human faces of poverty.

Poverty isn't just about material deprivation; it erodes hope, dignity, and the ability to reach one's full potential. It creates a vicious cycle, where limited resources hinder education and employment opportunities, perpetuating poverty across generations.

A Call to Understanding: Why We Need to Address Poverty

Poverty isn't a distant issue on a news report. It's a global challenge that impacts us all. A world riddled with poverty can breed instability, disease, and conflict. It's not just a moral imperative to address poverty, but a strategic necessity for a more peaceful and prosperous future.

This chapter is just the beginning. In the following chapters, we will delve deeper into the root causes of poverty, explore its impact on individuals and societies, and most importantly, discuss potential solutions and strategies to break the cycle. The fight against poverty requires a global effort, a collective understanding, and a commitment to building a world where everyone has the opportunity to thrive.

Beyond the Statistics: Stories of Struggle and Resilience

Numbers paint a grim picture, but poverty's true impact lies in the individual stories of struggle and resilience. Let's meet a few individuals whose lives exemplify the many faces of poverty:

- **Aisha, the Denied Education:** Aisha, a young girl from a remote village in India, dreams of becoming a doctor. However, her family can't afford to send her to school beyond primary education. Aisha faces a difficult choice: continue working in the fields with her family to barely scrape by, or defy tradition and fight for her education.

- **Miguel, the Trapped Laborer:** Miguel, a teenager in a Latin American city, works long hours in a sweatshop to contribute to his family's meager income. Despite the grueling conditions and low wages, Miguel feels trapped. He lacks the education and skills necessary to find better opportunities.

- **Sarah, the Single Mother:** Sarah, a single mother in a developed nation, juggles multiple low-paying jobs to make ends meet. Despite her hard work, she constantly struggles to afford childcare, healthy food, and decent housing. Sarah's story highlights how even in wealthy nations, structural inequalities can keep people trapped in poverty.

- **David, the Displaced Farmer:** David, a farmer in Africa, had to flee his home village due to a devastating drought. Climate change and unpredictable weather patterns have disrupted his livelihood, forcing him to start over in an unfamiliar city with scarce resources.

These are just a few snapshots of countless lives shaped by poverty. Each story is unique, but they all share a common thread: the desire for a better life, the struggle for basic necessities, and the hope for a brighter future.

The Ripple Effect: How Poverty Impacts Society as a Whole

Poverty doesn't exist in a vacuum. Its effects ripple outwards, impacting society as a whole.

- **Healthcare Burden:** Poor health outcomes are prevalent in poverty-stricken communities. Limited access to healthcare and preventative measures can lead to outbreaks of infectious diseases, further straining healthcare systems and resources.

- **Crime and Social Unrest:** Lack of opportunities and desperation can create fertile ground for crime. Furthermore, poverty can fuel social unrest and instability, posing a threat to overall security.

- **Economic Stagnation:** A large underemployed population can hinder economic growth. Poverty reduces the potential consumer base and limits the pool of skilled workers, slowing down economic development.

- **Lost Potential:** Poverty stifles creativity and innovation. When individuals struggle to meet basic needs, their talents and potential remain untapped, hindering societal progress.

A Call to Action: Breaking the Cycle of Poverty

The fight against poverty isn't just about charity; it's about empowering individuals and communities to break free from the cycle. It requires a multi-pronged approach, addressing education, healthcare, economic opportunities, and social justice issues.

Beyond Income: The Multidimensional Nature of Poverty

While income levels are crucial in defining poverty, they only tell part of the story. A concept gaining traction is **multidimensional poverty**, acknowledging that poverty encompasses various deprivations beyond just financial limitations. Here are some additional factors:

- **Lack of Access to Basic Services:** This includes clean water, sanitation facilities, reliable electricity, and safe housing. Many impoverished communities struggle to access these basic necessities, impacting their health and quality of life.

- **Social Exclusion and Discrimination:** Certain communities or groups might face marginalization based on ethnicity, caste, religion, or other factors. This exclusion can limit access to education, employment, and social services, perpetuating their disadvantaged position.

- **Food Insecurity:** Millions of people worldwide struggle to consistently access enough nutritious food. This can lead to malnutrition, stunted growth, and weakened immune systems, further hindering their ability to break free from poverty.

- **Limited Political Participation:** Poverty can impede opportunities for political participation. Without a voice in decision-making processes, impoverished communities have less power to advocate for their needs and challenge policies that perpetuate their struggles.

The Psychological Impact of Poverty:

Living in poverty can have a profound psychological impact. Individuals and families might experience chronic stress, anxiety, and depression. The constant struggle for basic needs can leave feelings of hopelessness and helplessness. Children raised in poverty might suffer from low self-esteem and experience learning difficulties.

A Global Issue, Local Realities:

While poverty is a global challenge, its manifestations differ significantly across regions. Here are a few examples:

- **Sub-Saharan Africa:** Extreme poverty rates remain high in many African countries, fueled by conflict, lack of infrastructure, and dependence on volatile commodity prices.

- **South Asia:** Large populations reside in rural areas with limited access to education and healthcare. Social inequalities based on caste and gender also play a significant role.

- **Developed Nations:** While income poverty is less prevalent, some demographics face significant challenges, such as single-parent households, minority groups experiencing discrimination, and the working poor who struggle to afford basic needs despite holding down jobs.

Looking Ahead

In the coming chapters, we will delve deeper into the causes and consequences of poverty, explore innovative solutions, and highlight inspiring stories of resilience and change. Let's move forward with a renewed sense of purpose, determined to build a world where everyone has the opportunity to reach their full potential and live a life free from poverty.

The Root Causes of Poverty

Chapter 1 painted a grim picture of poverty's many faces. Now, we delve into the tangled web of factors that contribute to this persistent global challenge. Understanding the root causes is crucial for crafting effective solutions.

A Systemic Issue: Lack of Education and Opportunity

According to The World Bank, one of the most significant drivers of poverty is a lack of access to quality education. Children raised in impoverished environments often lack the resources to attend school, hindering their ability to develop skills and gain knowledge necessary for future employment. This perpetuates the cycle, as uneducated parents are less likely to lift their children out of poverty. Furthermore, even if education is available, it may not be relevant to the job market. Rigid curriculums may not equip individuals with the skills needed for the changing economic landscape.

A Broken Ladder: Social Inequality and Injustice

Poverty isn't just about a lack of resources; it's also about social structures that perpetuate inequality. Unequal access to healthcare, proper sanitation, and clean water disproportionately affects impoverished communities.

Discriminatory policies and practices can further marginalize certain groups, making it even harder for them to climb the economic ladder. For example, women in some societies might face legal restrictions on property ownership or inheritance, limiting their economic independence.

Conflict, Violence, and Instability: A Vicious Cycle

Political instability and armed conflict act as potent catalysts for poverty. War destroys infrastructure, disrupts livelihoods, and forces populations to flee their homes. The psychological trauma associated with violence can also hinder people's ability to rebuild their lives. Furthermore, poverty itself can breed social unrest and violence. Frustration with limited opportunities and lack of basic necessities can create fertile ground for conflict and extremism.

Environmental Degradation: A Double-Edged Sword

The environment and poverty are inextricably linked. Climate change and environmental disasters disproportionately affect poor communities, destroying crops, displacing populations, and limiting access to resources. Poor communities might also be forced to exploit their environment to survive, leading to deforestation, soil degradation, and further ecological damage.

A Globalized Phenomenon: The Interconnected World

The globalized world creates a complex web of influences on poverty. While trade can offer opportunities for growth, it can also lead to job losses in certain sectors, particularly in developing countries. Economic policies implemented in one part of the world can have ripple effects on poverty rates in another.

The Role of Policy and Governance

The decisions made by governments and international institutions significantly impact poverty levels. Ineffective economic policies, corruption, and lack of transparency can stifle growth and exacerbate inequalities. On the other hand, sound policies aimed at promoting social justice, investing in education and healthcare, and fostering sustainable development can create a more level playing field and empower individuals to break free from poverty.

The Vicious Cycle of Debt

Debt can be a significant driver and consequence of poverty. Impoverished families often lack access to traditional banking systems and may resort to high-interest microloans to cover basic needs, emergencies, or investments in small businesses. However, the burden of high debt repayments can trap families in a cycle, where a significant portion of their income goes towards servicing debt instead of meeting essential needs or investing in the future.

Furthermore, predatory lending practices can exacerbate the situation. Lenders may exploit a lack of financial literacy among borrowers, leading to unsustainable debt burdens and asset stripping.

The Gender Gap in Poverty

Women and girls are disproportionately affected by poverty. Gender inequalities in education, employment opportunities, and property rights hinder their ability to earn a living and climb out of poverty. Additionally, women often shoulder the burden of unpaid care work, limiting their time for paid employment. Practices like child marriage and early pregnancy further limit opportunities for girls and perpetuate the cycle of poverty across generations.

The Challenge of Urbanization:

Rapid urbanization presents both opportunities and challenges when it comes to poverty. While cities offer access to jobs and services, they can also lead to overcrowded slums with inadequate housing, sanitation, and healthcare. Migrants from rural areas may struggle to find decent jobs and housing, particularly if they lack education or relevant skills.

The Private Sector and Corporate Practices

The private sector can play a significant role in both alleviating and exacerbating poverty. Unethical business practices, such as low wages, poor working conditions, and environmental exploitation, can contribute to poverty, particularly in developing countries.

However, businesses can also be a force for good. Fair trade practices, decent working conditions, and investments in local communities can empower people to lift themselves out of poverty. Additionally, the private sector can play a role in developing innovative solutions, such as mobile banking technologies that reach unbanked populations.

Chapter 2: The Root Causes of Poverty: A Tangled Web (Continued)

The Unseen Costs: The Psychological Impact of Poverty

While we often focus on the material deprivations associated with poverty, it's crucial to acknowledge the significant psychological impact it can have on individuals and communities. Living in poverty can be a constant source of stress and anxiety. The struggle to meet basic needs like food and shelter can leave people feeling overwhelmed and hopeless.

A Cycle of Learned Helplessness:

Chronic exposure to poverty can lead to a sense of learned helplessness. Individuals who experience repeated failures in securing employment or improving their situation may begin to believe they have no control over their circumstances. This can lead to a lack of motivation and a decreased capacity for future planning.

Mental Health Challenges:

Poverty is a significant risk factor for mental health problems such as depression and anxiety. The constant struggle for survival, coupled with limited access to mental healthcare, can create a vicious cycle. Mental health issues can further hinder individuals' ability to find and maintain employment, perpetuating poverty.

Impact on Children:

Children raised in poverty face a multitude of challenges. Experiencing food insecurity and inadequate housing can affect their physical and cognitive development. The stress and instability associated with poverty can also negatively impact their emotional well-being and academic performance.

Breaking the Cycle: Building Resilience and Hope

Despite these challenges, it's important to recognize the resilience of individuals and communities living in poverty. Social support systems, access to mental healthcare services, and educational programs that promote self-efficacy can empower people to overcome the psychological burdens of poverty and build a brighter future.

Looking Beyond Averages: The Heterogeneity of Poverty

Poverty isn't a uniform experience. Even within a single country or region, significant variations exist. Here are some factors that influence how poverty manifests differently:

- **Rural vs. Urban Poverty:** Challenges faced by poverty-stricken communities in rural areas differ from those in urban centers. Rural populations might struggle with limited access to infrastructure and services, while urban populations might contend with overcrowding and inadequate sanitation.

- **Gender and Age:** Women, children, and the elderly are often disproportionately affected by poverty due to societal inequalities and limited access to resources.

- **Ethnicity and Disability:** Discrimination based on ethnicity, race, or disability can create additional barriers to education and employment, exacerbating poverty.

The Paradox of Growth: Unequal Distribution of Benefits

Economic growth doesn't always translate to poverty reduction. In some cases, rapid economic development can exacerbate inequalities, leading to a phenomenon known as "unequal growth." This occurs when the benefits of economic growth are concentrated among a small segment of the population, while a large portion remains trapped in poverty. Factors that contribute to this include:

- **Lack of Trickle-Down Effect:** Economic growth doesn't always trickle down to reach the poorest segments of society. Job creation might be concentrated in sectors that require high levels of education and skills, leaving individuals with limited qualifications behind.

- **Resource Exploitation:** Unsustainable resource extraction practices to fuel economic growth might harm local communities and damage the environment, jeopardizing long-term livelihoods.

- **Political Capture:** Unequal distribution of political power can lead to policies that benefit the wealthy and powerful at the expense of the poor.

Globalization: A Double-Edged Sword

Globalization has had a complex impact on poverty. On the one hand, it has created opportunities for trade and investment, potentially leading to economic growth in developing countries. However, globalization can also have negative consequences:

- **Job Losses in Developed Countries:** Increased trade may lead to job losses in certain sectors of developed countries, as businesses relocate to take advantage of lower labor costs. This can disproportionately impact low-skilled workers.

- **Exploitation of Labor:** Globalization can create an environment where developing countries compete by offering low wages and lax labor regulations, potentially leading to exploitation of workers.

The Role of International Institutions

International institutions such as the World Bank and the International Monetary Fund (IMF) play a significant role in shaping economic policies of developing nations. Their lending practices and policy recommendations can influence poverty levels. Criticism towards these institutions often focuses on:

- **Structural Adjustment Programs:** These programs might impose austerity measures, leading to cuts in social welfare programs that further hurt the poor.

- **Focus on Economic Growth Over Equity:** Critics argue that some international institutions prioritize economic growth over social justice, neglecting the needs of the most vulnerable populations.

The root causes of poverty are a complex web of interrelated factors. It's not just about a lack of resources; it's about a lack of access to education, healthcare, and opportunities. Social inequality, political instability, environmental degradation, and the challenges of globalization all play a role.

Understanding these diverse and sometimes contradictory forces is crucial for crafting effective solutions. In the next chapter, we'll explore the global landscape of poverty and see how these root causes manifest in specific regions.

The Global Landscape of Poverty

Chapter 2 shed light on the tangled web of factors that contribute to poverty. Now, we embark on a global journey, exploring how poverty manifests differently across various regions. This exploration will paint a clearer picture of the diverse challenges and opportunities that exist across our interconnected world.

Sub-Saharan Africa: A Region in Transition

Sub-Saharan Africa remains the region with the highest poverty rates globally. Here are some key factors contributing to this challenge:

- **Conflict and Instability:** Civil wars, political instability, and violence disrupt livelihoods and displace populations, hindering economic development.

- **Dependence on Volatile Commodities:** Many African economies rely heavily on exports of raw materials like oil and minerals. Fluctuations in global commodity prices create economic instability, jeopardizing government revenue and social programs.

- **Weak Governance and Corruption:** Corruption and lack of transparency in governance can hinder economic growth and divert resources away from those who need them most.

- **Rapid Population Growth:** Rapid population growth can put a strain on resources and create challenges in providing education and healthcare services for all.

However, Sub-Saharan Africa also holds immense potential for growth. Entrepreneurship is on the rise, particularly among young people leveraging technology. Investments in infrastructure, education, and sustainable development offer promising pathways towards poverty reduction.

South Asia: Rural Challenges and Urban Growth

South Asia grapples with a significant rural-urban divide. Here's a breakdown of the challenges and opportunities:

- **Rural Poverty:** A large portion of the population resides in rural areas, facing limited access to education, healthcare, and infrastructure. Landlessness and dependence on rain-fed agriculture make them vulnerable to droughts and climate change.

- **Urbanization and Slums:** Rapid urbanization has created sprawling slums with inadequate sanitation, housing, and basic services. These informal settlements often lack access to formal employment opportunities.

- **Social Inequalities:** Caste systems and discriminatory practices based on gender and religion create barriers to education and employment for certain groups, perpetuating poverty.

Despite these challenges, South Asia also boasts a growing middle class and a vibrant civil society. Investments in rural development, education for girls, and skills training for urban populations can pave the way for a more equitable future.

Developed Nations: Pockets of Poverty in a Land of Plenty

While extreme poverty is less prevalent in developed nations, certain demographics still struggle significantly. Here are some key aspects to consider:

- **The Working Poor:** Low wages, combined with high costs of living, especially housing, can leave some working individuals and families struggling to meet basic needs.

- **Social Safety Nets:** The strength and accessibility of social safety nets like unemployment benefits and affordable housing programs significantly impact poverty rates.

- **Discrimination and Marginalization:** Minority groups and immigrants may face barriers to employment and housing due to discrimination, leading to higher poverty rates.

Developed nations have the resources and infrastructure to tackle poverty. Investing in affordable housing, raising minimum wages, and strengthening social safety nets are crucial steps towards ensuring everyone has the opportunity to thrive.

Emerging Economies: Balancing Growth and Equity

Rapid economic growth in emerging economies like those in Southeast Asia and Latin America offers opportunities for poverty reduction. However, challenges remain:

- **Income Inequality:** The benefits of economic growth may not be evenly distributed, creating pockets of extreme wealth alongside persistent poverty.

- **Informal Economy:** A large portion of the workforce might be employed in the informal sector, lacking job security and social safety net benefits.

- **Environmental Degradation:** Unsustainable development practices focused on rapid growth can have long-term consequences for livelihoods and resource availability.

Emerging economies face a crucial balancing act: sustaining economic growth while ensuring it benefits everyone. Investing in education, healthcare, and environmental protection will be crucial for creating a more inclusive and sustainable future.

Conclusion: A Global Challenge Demands a Global Response

Poverty doesn't respect national borders. The global landscape of poverty highlights its multifaceted nature and the diverse challenges faced by different regions. Understanding these regional disparities is crucial for crafting effective solutions and promoting international cooperation.

In the next chapter, we'll delve into the strategies and innovations that offer a glimmer of hope for a world free from poverty.

Beyond Statistics: Stories of Resilience and Hope

While statistics paint a sobering picture of poverty's global reach, it's the stories of resilience and hope that inspire action. Here are a few examples of how individuals and communities are overcoming poverty:

- **Microfinance: Empowering Entrepreneurs:** Microfinance institutions provide small loans to individuals, allowing them to start or expand their businesses. This approach empowers people to lift themselves out of poverty and contribute to their communities' economic growth.

• **Conditional Cash Transfers: Investing in Families' Futures:** Programs that provide direct cash transfers to families, often with conditions such as school attendance for children, can improve health outcomes, educational attainment, and overall well-being.

• **Mobile Banking: Reaching the Unbanked:** Technology can play a crucial role in financial inclusion. Mobile banking services allow people without access to traditional banks to manage finances, send and receive money, and access financial resources more easily.

• **Community-Driven Development:** According to the United Nations Sustainable Development Goals, Empowering local communities to identify their needs and develop solutions for poverty reduction is crucial for sustainability. This approach ensures solutions are tailored to specific contexts and foster a sense of ownership within communities.

Looking Ahead: Innovation for a More Equitable Future
The fight against poverty demands a multi-pronged approach, and innovation lies at the heart of progress. Here are some promising initiatives:

• **Social Impact Investing:** Investors are increasingly directing resources towards businesses and organizations that generate positive social and environmental impact alongside financial returns.

• **The Sharing Economy:** Platforms like ride-sharing and peer-to-peer accommodation can create income-generating opportunities for individuals while offering affordable services.

• **Social Entrepreneurship:** Businesses with a social mission are emerging, focused on creating sustainable solutions for poverty reduction, access to education, and healthcare.

The Role of Technology

Technology can be a powerful tool for empowering individuals and communities to overcome poverty. Here are some potential applications:

• **E-learning Platforms:** Digital platforms can offer access to educational resources and training opportunities in remote areas.

• **Telemedicine:** Technology can connect individuals in underserved areas with healthcare professionals, improving access to medical services.

• **Precision Agriculture** Data-driven farming techniques can help smallholder farmers optimize their yields and manage resources more efficiently.

The Specific Challenges Faced by Women and Girls

- **Gender Inequality:** Limited access to education, property rights, and reproductive healthcare disproportionately affect women and girls, hindering their ability to earn a living and escape poverty.

- **Child Marriage and Early Pregnancy:** These practices cut short girls' education and limit their future opportunities, perpetuating the cycle of poverty across generations.

- **Exploitative Labor:** Women and girls are particularly vulnerable to exploitation in the informal sector and global supply chains, often facing low wages and unsafe working conditions.

The Disproportionate Impact of Climate Change

- **Climate Disasters:** Extreme weather events like floods, droughts, and rising sea levels disproportionately impact impoverished communities, destroying crops, displacing populations, and eroding livelihoods.

- **Environmental Degradation:** Dependence on natural resources for subsistence living makes impoverished communities particularly vulnerable to environmental degradation, such as deforestation and desertification.

- **Resource Scarcity:** Climate change can exacerbate competition for scarce resources like water and arable land, leading to conflicts and further hardship for poor communities.

The Role of Conflict and Fragile States

- **Civil Wars and Political Instability:** These factors disrupt economies, destroy infrastructure, and displace populations, leading to a surge in poverty rates.

- **Weak Governance and Corruption:** Lack of transparency and accountability in government institutions can hinder aid effectiveness and create opportunities for corruption, diverting resources away from those who need them most.

- **Forced Displacement:** Millions of people worldwide are refugees or internally displaced persons due to conflict or persecution. These populations often face significant challenges in accessing basic necessities and rebuilding their lives.

By incorporating these aspects, Chapter 3 provides a more nuanced understanding of the global landscape of poverty and the diverse challenges faced by different groups and regions.

Empowering Change will explore specific actions individuals and organizations can take towards building a world free from poverty.

Empowering Change

According to the Poverty Action Lab, The fight against poverty is a complex challenge, but it's not insurmountable. Chapter 3 painted a picture of the diverse realities of poverty across the globe. Now, it's time to explore concrete actions individuals and organizations can take to empower change and build a world free from poverty.

Individual Action: Making a Difference in Your Sphere

- **Informed Consumerism:** Be mindful of the products you purchase and the companies you support. Choose brands committed to fair labor practices, sustainable sourcing, and social responsibility.

- **Advocacy and Awareness:** Raise awareness about poverty issues in your community and support organizations working towards solutions. Contact your elected officials and urge them to prioritize policies that address poverty's root causes.

- **Volunteer Your Time and Skills:** Volunteer your expertise to organizations working on poverty reduction initiatives. Donate to charities that align with your values and work directly with impoverished communities.

- **Live Mindfully:** Challenge your own biases and assumptions about poverty. Practice empathy and understanding towards those facing economic hardship.

Collective Action: The Power of Collaboration

- **Support Fair Trade Practices:** Choose products with fair trade certifications that ensure fair wages and safe working conditions for producers in developing countries.

- **Hold Corporations Accountable:** Demand transparency from corporations regarding their labor practices and environmental impact. Support initiatives that promote responsible corporate governance.

- **Engage in Citizen Science and Crowdfunding:** Participate in online platforms that allow individuals to contribute resources and knowledge to research projects addressing poverty-related issues.

The Role of Non-Profit Organizations

- **Community Development and Capacity Building:** Non-profits can empower local communities to identify their needs, develop solutions, and manage resources effectively.

- **Direct Service Provision:** Organizations can provide essential services such as healthcare, education, and legal aid to impoverished communities.

- **Advocacy and Policy Change:** Non-profits can work towards influencing policies at local, national, and international levels to address the structural barriers that perpetuate poverty.

The Role of Governments and International Institutions

• **Investing in Education and Healthcare:** Strong public education and healthcare systems are crucial for creating opportunities and improving the well-being of impoverished populations.

• **Promoting Social Safety Nets:** Social safety nets such as unemployment benefits and affordable housing programs can provide a vital safety net for those facing economic hardship.

• **Foreign Aid with Accountability:** Ensure that foreign aid is directed towards sustainable development projects and reaches the intended beneficiaries. Implement mechanisms to monitor aid effectiveness and prevent corruption.

• **Debt Relief and Fair Trade Agreements:** Consider debt relief programs for developing countries and negotiate trade agreements that promote fair trade practices and sustainable development.

The Power of Innovation and Technology

• **Promoting Social Entrepreneurship:** Support innovative businesses with a social mission that create solutions for poverty reduction, access to education, and healthcare.

• **Investing in Digital Infrastructure and Education:** Expand access to technology and provide digital literacy training in impoverished communities.

- **Leveraging Technology for Financial Inclusion:** Promote mobile banking and other digital financial services to reach the unbanked population and facilitate financial empowerment.

Chapter 4 has reached a strong conclusion, but we can add some elements to further inspire action:

Chapter 4: A Call to Action: Empowering Change (Continued)
Beyond Charity: Building Sustainable Solutions
While traditional charity plays a role, a focus on sustainable solutions is crucial for long-term poverty reduction. Here's the shift in perspective:

- **From Handouts to Hand-Ups:** Empowering individuals and communities to develop skills, access resources, and build their own livelihoods is more effective than simply providing temporary assistance.

- **Investing in Education and Skills Development:** Education is the key to unlocking opportunities and breaking the cycle of poverty. Investing in quality education and relevant skills training empowers individuals to secure better jobs and build a brighter future.

- **Promoting Gender Equality and Women's Empowerment:** When women have equal access to education, healthcare, and economic opportunities, they can contribute more effectively to their families' and communities' well-being.

- **Promoting Sustainable Development:** Environmental sustainability is intertwined with poverty reduction. Investing in renewable energy, sustainable agriculture, and climate-resilient infrastructure creates jobs and ensures long-term resource availability for future generations.

The Importance of Storytelling and Changing the Narrative

Poverty is often portrayed through a lens of helplessness. Countering this narrative is crucial for inspiring action:

- **Sharing Stories of Resilience:** Highlighting the stories of individuals and communities overcoming poverty can inspire hope and demonstrate the power of human potential.

- **Shifting the Focus to Dignity and Empowerment:** Framing poverty reduction as a matter of human rights and dignity, rather than just charity, fosters a sense of shared responsibility and collective action.

Staying Motivated and Engaged in the Long Haul

The fight against poverty is a marathon, not a sprint. Here's how to stay motivated:

- **Celebrate Progress, Big and Small:** Acknowledge and celebrate successes, no matter how small. Every step forward, every life improved, is a victory.

- **Connect with a Cause You Care About:** Find a specific issue related to poverty reduction that resonates with you and focus your efforts there. Passion fuels long-term commitment.

• **Build a Support Network:** Connect with others who share your passion for creating change. A supportive network can provide encouragement, share resources, and prevent burnout.

Remember, change starts with a single step. Let's all take that step together!

Chapter 4 outlined a powerful call to action for individuals and organizations. Now, let's delve into the crucial role businesses can play in the fight against poverty. Traditionally, the focus has been on maximizing profit, but a growing movement emphasizes businesses as forces for good, integrating social responsibility and environmental sustainability into their core practices.

Beyond the Bottom Line: The Rise of Social Impact Businesses

Social impact businesses are a new wave of companies that prioritize positive social and environmental impact alongside financial returns. Here are some key models:

- **Benefit Corporations:** These legal entities formally commit to balancing profit with social and environmental objectives.

- **Social Enterprises:** These businesses reinvest profits into their social mission, aiming to address specific needs within communities.

- **Fair Trade Businesses:** These companies ensure fair wages and ethical treatment for producers in developing countries.

Integrating Social Responsibility Throughout the Value Chain

Businesses can create positive social impact by considering these aspects:

- **Ethical Sourcing:** Ensuring fair labor practices, safe working conditions, and environmental sustainability throughout their supply chains.

- **Living Wages:** Committing to paying a living wage that allows employees to meet their basic needs and participate in the local economy.

- **Community Development:** Investing in initiatives that improve the lives of people in the communities where they operate, such as education programs or healthcare facilities.

Examples of Business as a Force for Good

Here are a few examples of how businesses are making a difference:

- **Grameen Bank:** This micro finance institution in Bangladesh provides small loans to impoverished women, empowering them to start businesses and lift themselves out of poverty.

- **Patagonia:** This outdoor clothing company is a leader in environmental sustainability, using recycled materials and advocating for environmental protection.

- **TOMS Shoes:** For every pair of shoes they sell, TOMS donates a pair to a child in need.

The Challenges and Opportunities of Social Impact

While exciting opportunities exist, challenges remain:

- **Measuring Impact:** Quantifying the social impact of business activities can be complex and requires robust measurement frameworks.

- **Balancing Profit and Purpose:** Some argue that focusing on social responsibility can detract from profitability. However, strong evidence suggests that companies with strong social responsibility practices attract and retain talent, build brand loyalty, and ultimately improve their bottom line.

- **Consumer Awareness:** Consumers need to be aware of companies that are truly committed to social responsibility and make informed choices when purchasing products and services.

The Future of Work: Automation and the Rise of the Gig Economy

According to the Center for Global Development, technological advancements are rapidly transforming the job market. Automation threatens to displace workers in certain sectors, while the gig economy offers new opportunities alongside challenges. Here's a breakdown:

- **Automation and Job Displacement:** Certain repetitive tasks are increasingly being automated, raising concerns about job losses in specific sectors like manufacturing and transportation.

- **The Rise of the Gig Economy:** Platforms like Uber and Lyft have created a surge in gig work, characterized by short-term contracts and independent work arrangements. This offers flexibility for workers, but often lacks benefits and job security.

Navigating the Changing Landscape

To ensure a just transition in the face of automation, a focus on training the workforce is crucial. Here are some strategies:

- **Government Initiatives:** Governments can invest in training programs that equip workers with the skills needed for jobs in the digital age.

- **Corporate Responsibility:** Businesses can offer training opportunities to their employees and invest in programs that prepare workers for the changing job market.

- **Educational Reform:** Educational systems need to adapt to equip students with the skills and adaptability needed to thrive in the future of work.

Promoting Inclusive Growth: Bridging the Digital Divide

The digital divide – the gap in access to information and communication technologies – can exacerbate inequalities in the future of work. Here's how to address it:

- **Expanding Access to Technology:** Initiatives to provide affordable internet access and digital literacy training, particularly in underserved communities, are crucial.

- **Digital Skills Development:** Equipping individuals with the necessary digital skills to participate in the digital economy allows them to access a wider range of job opportunities.

The Role of Social Safety Nets

In a world with a changing job market, strong social safety nets become even more critical:

- **Unemployment Benefits:** Adequate unemployment benefits can provide a temporary safety net for individuals who lose their jobs due to automation or other factors.

- **Universal Basic Income (UBI):** The concept of a UBI, a guaranteed income for all citizens, is gaining traction as a way to address income inequality and provide a safety net in the future of work.

Beyond Traditional Employment: The Potential of Social Entrepreneurship

While social responsibility within established businesses is crucial, social entrepreneurship offers another powerful approach. Social entrepreneurs are individuals who create businesses with a social mission, aiming to address specific needs within communities and create positive social change. Here are some key aspects:

- **Innovative Solutions for Poverty Reduction:** Social entrepreneurs develop innovative businesses that address issues like lack of access to education, healthcare, or clean water.

- **Creating Sustainable Impact:** Social enterprises aim to create long-term, sustainable solutions that empower communities and address the root causes of poverty.

- **Building a Market for Good:** Social entrepreneurship encourages investment in businesses that generate both social and financial returns.

The Role of Business in Promoting Financial Inclusion

Financial inclusion is crucial for poverty reduction. Businesses can play a role in:

- **Mobile Banking and Financial Technology (FinTech):** Supporting the development and accessibility of mobile banking and financial services allows individuals in underserved communities to manage their finances and access credit more easily.

- **Microfinance Institutions:** Partnering with or investing in micro finance institutions that provide small loans to impoverished individuals, enabling them to start or expand businesses.

- **Financial Literacy Programs:** Collaborating on initiatives that educate individuals about managing their finances, making informed investment decisions, and saving for the future.

Consumer Power and Ethical Choices

Consumers hold significant power in influencing corporate behavior. Here's how:

- **Supporting Businesses with Strong Social Responsibility Practices:** By consciously choosing brands committed to fair labor practices, ethical sourcing, and environmental sustainability, consumers encourage businesses to prioritize social good.

- **Demanding Transparency and Accountability:** Consumers can hold businesses accountable for their social and environmental impact by demanding transparency in their practices.

- **Advocating for Change:** Consumers can use their collective voice to advocate for policies that promote ethical business practices and hold corporations accountable for their impact on society.

Conclusion: A Multi-Stakeholder Approach Towards a More Equitable Future

The fight against poverty demands a multi-stakeholder approach. Businesses have a crucial role to play by integrating social responsibility into their core operations, fostering financial inclusion, and responding to consumer demands for ethical practices.

By collaborating with governments, NGOs, and empowered consumers, businesses can leverage their resources and influence to create a more equitable future where economic growth benefits everyone.

The next chapter will explore the power of youth: how young people are driving innovation and change in the fight against poverty.

Throughout history, young people have been at the forefront of social movements and positive change. In the fight against poverty, their energy, creativity, and idealism are a driving force. This chapter explores the diverse ways young people are making a difference and shaping a brighter future.

Young Minds, Big Dreams: Leading with Innovation

Young people are uniquely positioned to contribute fresh perspectives and innovative ideas to tackle complex problems like poverty. Here are some examples:

- **Tech for Good Initiatives:** Young developers are creating apps and online platforms that address issues like access to education, healthcare, and financial services in underserved communities.

- **Social Entrepreneurship:** Across the globe, young people are launching businesses with a social mission, providing solutions for challenges like clean water access, sustainable agriculture, and affordable housing.

- **Youth-Led Advocacy:** Young activists are raising awareness about poverty-related issues and advocating for policy changes that promote social justice and economic opportunity.

Harnessing the Power of Social Media:

Social media has become a powerful tool for young people to connect, mobilize, and drive change:

- **Raising Awareness:** Young people use social media to share stories, statistics, and calls to action regarding poverty, sparking conversations and inspiring others to get involved.

- **Crowdfunding and Fundraising Platforms:** Social media allows young people to raise funds for causes they care about, supporting projects and initiatives working towards poverty reduction.

- **Building Online Communities:** Social media platforms provide a space for young people to connect with others passionate about addressing poverty, share knowledge, and collaborate on solutions.

Breaking Down Barriers: Empowering Others
Young people can be powerful agents of change within their own communities:

- **Mentorship Programs:** Young adults can mentor younger students, providing guidance, support, and inspiration to help them reach their full potential.

- **Community Service Initiatives:** Volunteering for local organizations that provide services to impoverished communities is a way for young people to make a direct impact and learn about the realities of poverty firsthand.

- **Peer Education:** Young people can educate their peers about poverty-related issues, fostering empathy and encouraging them to get involved in finding solutions.

Examples of Young Leaders Making a Difference

Here are a few examples of inspiring young leaders making a difference in the fight against poverty:

- **Malala Yousafzai:** An advocate for girls' education, Malala spoke out against the Taliban's ban on girls' education in Pakistan. She received the Nobel Peace Prize at age 17, becoming the youngest Nobel laureate.

- **Greta Thunberg:** This young climate activist has led a global movement demanding action on climate change, highlighting the connection between environmental degradation and poverty.

- **Kelvin Doe:** At age 13, this Sierra Leonean boy built a generator out of scrap materials. He has gone on to become an innovator and advocate for STEM education in his country.

Challenges and Opportunities

Despite their enthusiasm and potential, young people also face challenges:

- **Limited Resources and Funding:** Young activists and social entrepreneurs often lack the resources and financial backing necessary to support their initiatives.

- **Lack of Experience and Access:** Young people may lack the experience and established networks to navigate the complex world of policy change and large-scale projects.

- **Combating Discouragement:** The vastness of poverty can be overwhelming. Mentorship and support systems are crucial to maintain motivation and hope.

Investing in the Future: Supporting Young Leaders
To unleash the full potential of young people in the fight against poverty, specific measures are needed:

- **Mentorship and Training Programs:** Providing young leaders with mentorship opportunities and training programs can equip them with the skills and knowledge to navigate complex challenges.

- **Funding and Resource Allocation:** Investing in youth-led initiatives, providing access to grants, and creating platforms for crowdfunding can empower young people to turn their ideas into reality.

- **Amplifying Youth Voices:** Creating platforms for young people to share their ideas, concerns, and solutions ensures their voices are heard by decision-makers.

Beyond Individual Action: The Power of Youth Movements
Young people have a long history of organizing and mobilizing for social change. Here's the strength of youth movements:

- **Collective Action and Amplifying Voices:** Youth movements create a powerful force for change by uniting young people around a common cause. Their collective voice demands attention and can influence policy decisions.

- **Grassroots Initiatives and Local Solutions:** Young people are often well-positioned to understand the specific needs of their communities and develop solutions that address local challenges related to poverty.

- **Creativity, Disruption, and Holding Power to Account:** Youth movements are known for their creative approaches to advocacy and their willingness to challenge the status quo. This can be a powerful tool for holding institutions accountable.

Examples of Powerful Youth Movements

Throughout history, youth movements have played a pivotal role in social progress:

- **The Civil Rights Movement:** Young people were at the forefront of the fight for racial equality in the United States during the 1950s and 1960s. Leaders like Martin Luther King Jr. and Rosa Parks mobilized millions and helped dismantle segregationist laws.

- **The Arab Spring:** In 2010, youth across the Middle East and North Africa used social media to organize protests against authoritarian regimes, demanding democracy and social justice.

- **The Climate Change Movement:** Greta Thunberg's Fridays for Future movement is a prime example of young people mobilizing on a global scale to demand action on climate change, a major factor contributing to poverty.

The Importance of Intergenerational Collaboration

While youth movements are a powerful force, collaboration is key:

Bridging the Knowledge Gap: Experienced individuals can provide valuable mentorship, guidance, and historical context to youth activists.

Sharing Resources and Strategies: Collaboration allows for the sharing of resources, skills, and established networks between generations of activists.

Building a Sustainable Movement: Intergenerational collaboration ensures the movement's longevity and the transfer of knowledge and experience to future generations.

The Vicious Cycle: Poverty's Impact on Mental Health

Poverty and mental health have a complex, intertwined relationship. Poverty can be both a cause and a consequence of mental health issues:

Chronic Stress and Anxiety: Living in poverty creates constant stress due to concerns about basic needs like food, shelter, and healthcare. This chronic stress can lead to anxiety disorders and depression.

Exposure to Trauma: Poverty often exposes individuals to traumatic experiences like violence, neglect, and social exclusion, increasing the risk of developing Post-Traumatic Stress Disorder (PTSD) and other mental health conditions.

Limited Access to Mental Health Services: People living in poverty often lack access to affordable and quality mental health services, which can further exacerbate existing problems.

Mental Health Challenges Faced by Young People in Poverty
Young people living in poverty are particularly vulnerable:

Academic Difficulties: Mental health challenges can hinder a young person's ability to learn and thrive in school, perpetuating the cycle of poverty.

Social Isolation and Stigma: Mental health conditions can lead to social isolation and stigma, further marginalizing young people from their peers and communities.

Substance Abuse: Some young people in poverty may turn to substance abuse as a way to cope with their struggles, leading to additional problems.

Breaking the Cycle: Promoting Mental Wellbeing

Fortunately, there are ways to break this cycle and promote mental wellbeing among young people living in poverty:

Integrating Mental Health Support into Anti-Poverty Programs: Anti-poverty programs should incorporate mental health services to address the emotional and psychological needs of individuals and families.

School-Based Interventions: Schools can play a crucial role in identifying mental health challenges in young people and providing support services.

Building Resilience and Coping Skills: Equipping young people with coping skills and fostering resilience can help them manage stress and navigate challenges more effectively.

Combatting Stigma: Educational campaigns and awareness programs can help reduce the stigma surrounding mental health, encouraging young people to seek help.

The Role of Young People in Promoting Mental Wellbeing

Young people can also play a vital role in promoting mental wellbeing within their communities:

Supporting Peers: Educate each other about mental health, and create a safe space for open communication about mental health challenges.

Advocating for Change: Young people can speak up about the need for greater access to mental health services and advocate for policies that support mental wellbeing.

Breaking the Stigma: By openly talking about mental health, young people can help challenge the stigma and normalize seeking help when needed.

The Vicious Cycle: Poverty's Impact on Mental Health

Poverty and mental health have a complex, intertwined relationship. Poverty can be both a cause and a consequence of mental health issues:

- **Chronic Stress and Anxiety:** Living in poverty creates constant stress due to concerns about basic needs like food, shelter, and healthcare. This chronic stress can lead to anxiety disorders and depression.

- **Exposure to Trauma:** Poverty often exposes individuals to traumatic experiences like violence, neglect, and social exclusion, increasing the risk of developing Post-Traumatic Stress Disorder (PTSD) and other mental health conditions.

- **Limited Access to Mental Health Services:** People living in poverty often lack access to affordable and quality mental health services, which can further exacerbate existing problems.

Mental Health Challenges Faced by Young People in Poverty
Young people living in poverty are particularly vulnerable:

- **Academic Difficulties:** Mental health challenges can hinder a young person's ability to learn and thrive in school, perpetuating the cycle of poverty.

- **Social Isolation and Stigma:** Mental health conditions can lead to social isolation and stigma, further marginalizing young people from their peers and communities.

- **Substance Abuse:** Some young people in poverty may turn to substance abuse as a way to cope with their struggles, leading to additional problems.

Breaking the Cycle: Promoting Mental Wellbeing

Fortunately, there are ways to break this cycle and promote mental wellbeing among young people living in poverty:

- **Integrating Mental Health Support into Anti-Poverty Programs:** Anti-poverty programs should incorporate mental health services to address the emotional and psychological needs of individuals and families.

- **School-Based Interventions:** Schools can play a crucial role in identifying mental health challenges in young people and providing support services.

- **Building Resilience and Coping Skills:** Equipping young people with coping skills and fostering resilience can help them manage stress and navigate challenges more effectively.

- **Combatting Stigma:** Educational campaigns and awareness programs can help reduce the stigma surrounding mental health, encouraging young people to seek help.

The Role of Young People in Promoting Mental Wellbeing

Young people can also play a vital role in promoting mental wellbeing within their communities:

- **Supporting Peers:** Educate each other about mental health, and create a safe space for open communication about mental health challenges.

- **Advocating for Change:** Young people can speak up about the need for greater access to mental health services and advocate for policies that support mental wellbeing.

- **Breaking the Stigma:** By openly talking about mental health, young people can help challenge the stigma and normalize seeking help when needed.

Stories of Hope and Resilience: The Power of Positive Role Models

Young people living in poverty often lack positive role models who have overcome similar challenges. Here's how stories and role models can inspire:

- **Sharing Success Stories:** Highlighting the stories of young people who have overcome poverty and mental health challenges can inspire others and demonstrate the power of resilience.

- **Mentorship Programs with Mentally Healthy Role Models:** Connecting young people with mentors who have navigated similar struggles and prioritize mental wellbeing can provide valuable guidance and support.

- **Positive Media Representation:** Promoting positive media portrayals of young people living in poverty who are actively working towards a better future can challenge stereotypes and inspire hope.

By sharing stories of hope and resilience, and showcasing successful young people who prioritize mental wellbeing, we can empower others to break the cycle of poverty and mental health challenges. This concludes Chapter 6: The Power of Youth: Agents of Change. We've explored the diverse ways young people are driving change, the challenges they face, and the importance of addressing mental health. The next chapter will shift focus to the broader issue of mental health for all, exploring its significance for a sustainable future.

A Cornerstone of Sustainable Development

Throughout this exploration of poverty, we've delved into its root causes, the fight for economic justice, and the crucial role of young people. Now, let's shift our focus to a fundamental aspect often overlooked in discussions of poverty reduction: mental health.

Beyond Material Needs: The Importance of Mental Wellbeing

While economic security is essential, a focus solely on material needs paints an incomplete picture. Mental health is a crucial component of individual and collective well-being. Here's why it matters:

- **Improved Quality of Life:** Good mental health allows individuals to live fulfilling lives, maintain healthy relationships, and contribute meaningfully to their communities.

- **Increased Productivity:** Mental health challenges can have a significant impact on an individual's ability to work and be productive. Conversely, good mental health fosters a more productive workforce.

- **Reduced Healthcare Costs:** Addressing mental health issues proactively can prevent more serious problems and reduce the overall healthcare burden.

- **Breaking the Cycle of Poverty:** Mental health challenges can perpetuate the cycle of poverty, while good mental wellbeing empowers individuals to escape poverty and reach their full potential.

The Global Mental Health Landscape: Challenges and Opportunities

Mental health challenges are a global concern, but the landscape varies across regions:

- **Limited Access to Care:** Many regions lack sufficient mental health professionals and resources, creating a significant treatment gap.

- **Stigma and Discrimination:** Stigma surrounding mental illness is a significant barrier to seeking help, preventing individuals from receiving the support they need.

- **The Impact of Conflict and Trauma:** War, civil unrest, and natural disasters can have a lasting impact on mental health, requiring specialized services.

Despite the challenges, significant opportunities exist:

- **Increased Awareness and Advocacy:** Mental health awareness campaigns are helping to reduce stigma and encourage individuals to seek help.

- **Technological Advancements:** Telehealth and online resources are providing greater access to mental health services in underserved areas.

- **The Rise of Community-Based Interventions:** Community-based initiatives are offering culturally relevant and accessible mental health support.

The Role of Governments and International Organizations
Governments and international organizations can play a vital role in promoting mental health for all:

- **Increased Investment in Mental Health Services:** Increased funding for mental health services is crucial for expanding access to care and improving service quality.

- **Mental Health Policy Development:** Developing comprehensive mental health policies that prioritize prevention, treatment, and rehabilitation is essential.

- **Training and Support for Mental Health Professionals:** Investing in training and support programs for mental health professionals ensures the availability of a qualified workforce.

Individual and Community Action: Empowering Change
Beyond policy changes, individual and community action plays a crucial role:

- **Combating Stigma:** Open conversations about mental health can help to normalize seeking help and reduce stigma.

- **Promoting Self-Care Practices:** Developing healthy coping mechanisms and prioritizing self-care can promote mental wellbeing

- **Creating Supportive Communities:** Building strong social connections and fostering a sense of belonging can have a positive impact on mental health.

Mental Health in a Changing World

The challenges and opportunities for mental health will continue to evolve alongside our changing world:

- **The Impact of Technology:** Technology can be a powerful tool for promoting mental health through online resources and support communities. However, it's crucial to address potential downsides like social media addiction and cyberbullying.

- **Climate Change and Environmental Degradation:** The mental health impacts of climate change, such as anxiety and displacement, require innovative interventions and support systems.

- **The Future of Work:** The changing nature of work, with automation and potential job displacement, necessitates mental health support for individuals navigating career transitions.

A Call to Action: Building a More Supportive World

Here are some key actions we can take to build a world that prioritizes mental health:

- **Cross-Sector Collaboration:** Governments, businesses, NGOs, and community organizations need to work together to develop comprehensive mental health strategies.

- **Equity and Inclusion:** Mental health services and resources must be accessible to everyone, regardless of race, ethnicity, socioeconomic background, or sexual orientation.

- **Investing in Youth Mental Health:** Promoting mental wellbeing from a young age sets individuals up for success and reduces long-term problems.

- **Breaking Down Silos:** Mental health needs to be integrated into broader conversations about healthcare, education, and social justice.

Chapter 7: Mental Health for All: A Cornerstone of Sustainable Development (Continued)

Chapter 7 has highlighted the critical importance of mental health for individual and collective well-being. Let's explore some additional considerations for building a future where mental health is a priority for all.

Mental Health in a Changing World

The challenges and opportunities for mental health will continue to evolve alongside our changing world:

- **The Impact of Technology:** Technology can be a powerful tool for promoting mental health through online resources and support communities. However, it's crucial to address potential downsides like social media addiction and cyberbullying.

- **Climate Change and Environmental Degradation:** The mental health impacts of climate change, such as anxiety and displacement, require innovative interventions and support systems.

- **The Future of Work:** The changing nature of work, with automation and potential job displacement, necessitates mental health support for individuals navigating career transitions.

A Call to Action: Building a More Supportive World

Here are some key actions we can take to build a world that prioritizes mental health:

- **Cross-Sector Collaboration:** Governments, businesses, NGOs, and community organizations need to work together to develop comprehensive mental health strategies.

- **Equity and Inclusion:** Mental health services and resources must be accessible to everyone, regardless of race, ethnicity, socioeconomic background, or sexual orientation.

- **Investing in Youth Mental Health:** Promoting mental wellbeing from a young age sets individuals up for success and reduces long-term problems.

- **Breaking Down Silos:** Mental health needs to be integrated into broader conversations about healthcare, education, and social justice.

Conclusion: A Message of Hope for the Future

The fight against poverty and the pursuit of mental health for all are complex challenges. However, there is reason for hope. With increased awareness, growing investment, and a commitment to collaborative action, we can create a future where everyone has the opportunity to reach their full potential and live a fulfilling life.

By prioritizing mental health, we can foster stronger communities, build a more equitable world, and ensure a more sustainable future for generations to come. This concludes our exploration of poverty and its multifaceted dimensions.

Chapter 9: The Gender Dimension of Poverty

Poverty doesn't affect everyone equally. Women and girls often experience poverty differently and more acutely than men and boys. This chapter explores the specific challenges faced by women living in poverty and how we can empower them for economic participation and social mobility.

The Unequal Burden: Understanding Gender Disparities

- **Limited Access to Education and Skills Development:** Girls are often denied access to education, limiting their career opportunities and earning potential.

- **Unpaid Care Work:** Women disproportionately shoulder the burden of unpaid care work, like childcare and housework, hindering their ability to participate in the formal workforce.

- **Discrimination and Gender Norms:** Social norms and gender biases can limit women's property rights, inheritance, and access to financial services, hindering their economic independence.

- **Gender-Based Violence:** Poverty can increase vulnerability to violence and exploitation, furthering marginalization.

Breaking the Cycle: Strategies for Empowering Women

Despite the challenges, there are strategies to empower women and break the cycle of poverty:

- **Investing in Girls' Education:** Ensuring access to quality education for girls is crucial for their future economic opportunities and overall well-being.

- **Promoting Skills Development and Vocational Training:** Providing women with relevant skills training empowers them to enter the workforce and secure decent jobs.

- **Microfinance and Financial Inclusion:** Microfinance programs and access to financial services can enable women to start small businesses and gain financial independence.

- **Supporting Women's Land Rights and Property Ownership:** Securing land and property rights for women empowers them to participate in agricultural production and make economic decisions.

- **Addressing Gender-Based Violence:** Combating violence and promoting women's safety is essential for their overall empowerment.

- **Promoting Inclusive Policies and Legislation:** Policies that address gender pay gaps, parental leave, and childcare support can level the playing field for women.

Women as Agents of Change: Examples of Success

Women are not just passive victims of poverty; they are also powerful agents of change:

- **Women-Led Businesses:** Supporting women entrepreneurs and fostering women-owned businesses can stimulate economic growth and create jobs.

- **Community Leadership:** Empowering women to participate in community decision-making processes ensures their voices are heard and their needs are addressed.

- **Grassroots Movements:** Women-led social movements are actively fighting for gender equality and advocating for policies that benefit women living in poverty.

Chapter 9: The Gender Dimension of Poverty (Continued)

Empowering women requires a multifaceted approach that goes beyond economic initiatives. Here's a deeper dive into some crucial aspects:

Shifting Social Norms and Attitudes:

- **Education Campaigns:** Raising awareness about gender equality and challenging traditional gender roles through educational campaigns can create a more supportive environment for women's empowerment.

- **Engaging Men and Boys:** Including men and boys in conversations about gender equality and promoting their role in dismantling patriarchal structures is crucial for long-term change.

- **Role Models and Mentorship:** Showcasing successful women leaders and entrepreneurs can inspire young girls and demonstrate the possibilities available to them.

Addressing Health and Reproductive Rights:

- **Maternal Health Services:** Ensuring access to quality maternal healthcare is essential for women's well-being and reduces risks associated with childbirth, particularly in low-resource settings.

- **Family Planning:** Providing access to family planning services empowers women to make informed choices about their reproductive health, allowing them to plan their families and pursue education and economic opportunities.

- **Combating Gender-Based Violence:** Providing safe spaces, legal support, and resources for survivors of violence is essential for women's physical and mental well-being.

The Role of Technology:

- **Financial Technology (FinTech):** Mobile banking and digital financial services can provide women with secure financial tools and overcome traditional barriers to accessing financial services.

- **Education and Training Platforms:** Online learning platforms can offer women access to educational resources and skills development opportunities, regardless of location.

• **Communication and Networking Tools:** Technology can connect women entrepreneurs and farmers to markets, information, and support networks.

Conclusion: A Call to Action

Empowering women is a collective responsibility. Governments, international organizations, civil society, and the private sector all have a role to play. Individuals can also contribute by:

• **Supporting businesses owned by women.**

• **Challenging gender stereotypes in everyday life.**

• **Advocating for policies that promote gender equality.**

• **Sponsoring a girl's education or donating to organizations that empower women.**

By working together, we can create a world where women have the opportunities and resources to reach their full potential and contribute to a more prosperous and equitable future for all.

This concludes Chapter 9: The Gender Dimension of Poverty.

Throughout this journey, we've explored the complex realities of poverty, its root causes, and the inspiring efforts to create a more just and equitable world. We've delved into the power of individuals, communities, and collective action. As we reach the conclusion of this book, it's time to reflect on the path forward and the future we can build together.

From Knowledge to Action: Building a More Equitable World

Eradicating poverty is not an impossible dream. The knowledge and tools exist to create a world where everyone has the opportunity to thrive. However, achieving this goal requires a paradigm shift:

- **Moving Beyond Charity:** While charity has a role to play, a focus on sustainable solutions that address the root causes of poverty is more effective in the long run.

- **Building Inclusive Systems:** Economic and social systems need to be designed to include everyone, regardless of background or circumstance. This means investing in education, healthcare, and social safety nets.

- **Global Partnership:** Poverty eradication is a global challenge. Developed and developing countries must work together to share resources, knowledge, and best practices.

- **Empowering Individuals and Communities:** Sustainable solutions require the active participation of people living in poverty. Community-driven development ensures that interventions are culturally appropriate and address local needs.

The Power of Hope and Inspiration

The fight against poverty can be daunting, but it is also a journey filled with hope and inspiration. Here's what gives us reason to believe in a brighter future:

- **The Resilience of the Human Spirit:** Despite immense challenges, people living in poverty demonstrate extraordinary resilience and a desire to build a better future for themselves and their families.

- **The Power of Innovation:** Technology and innovation offer new tools for tackling poverty, from financial inclusion to remote learning opportunities.

- **The Rise of Global Consciousness:** There's a growing global awareness of the issue of poverty and a willingness to take action for change.

A Call to Action: Building a Future Where No One is Left Behind

Eradicating poverty requires action from everyone – individuals, businesses, governments, and civil society organizations. Here are some specific ways you can contribute:

- **Advocate for Policies that Promote Economic Inclusion:** Support policies that create decent jobs, invest in social safety nets, and ensure equitable access to education and healthcare.

- **Make Conscious Consumer Choices:** Support businesses that prioritize ethical practices, fair trade, and sustainable sourcing.

- **Volunteer Your Time and Skills:** Donate your time or expertise to organizations working to alleviate poverty in your community or globally.

- **Raise Awareness:** Educate yourself and others about the issue of poverty and inspire action in your networks.

- **Live a Life of Compassion and Solidarity:** Empathy and a commitment to building a more just and equitable world are essential for lasting change.

The future we create is a choice. By working together with compassion, innovation, and a commitment to shared prosperity, we can build a world where poverty is a relic of the past. Let's ensure that future generations inherit a world where everyone has the opportunity to thrive and reach their full potential.

This marks the conclusion of this book on poverty. Remember, the journey towards a more just world begins with a single step. Take action today and be a part of the solution.

Thank You

Sincerely, Tyler

- **The World Bank:** https://data.worldbank.org/topic/poverty

- **The United Nations Sustainable Development Goals:** https://sdgs.un.org/goals

- **The Brookings Institution:** https://www.brookings.edu/

- **The Center for Global Development:** https://www.cgdev.org/

- **The Poverty Action Lab:** https://www.povertyactionlab.org/